Pearson

Year 4

Grammar and Punctuation
Activity Workbook

Author:
Hannah
Hirst-Dunton

Published by Pearson Education Limited, 80 Strand, London, WC2R 0RL.
www.pearsonschools.co.uk

Text © Pearson Education Limited 2022
Edited by Florence Production Ltd
Designed by Pearson Education Limited 2022
Typeset by Florence Production Ltd
Produced by Florence Production Ltd and Sarah Loader
Original illustrations © Pearson Education Limited 2022
Cover design by Pearson Education Limited 2022

The right of Hannah Hirst-Dunton to be identified as author of this work has been asserted by her in accordance with the Copyright, Designs and Patents Act 1988.

First published 2022

25 24 23 22
10 9 8 7 6 5 4 3 2 1

British Library Cataloguing in Publication Data
A catalogue record for this book is available from the British Library

ISBN 978 1 292 425009

Printed in Slovakia by Neografia

Acknowledgements
Front Cover: Lauren Murray/Shutterstock; Anna Frajtova/Shutterstock; Neonic Flower/Shutterstock.

The author and publisher would like to thank the following individuals and organisations for permission to reproduce photographs:

(Key: b-bottom; c-centre; l-left; r-right; t-top)

Shutterstock: Olga Utchenko iv, 16, 21, 31, 45, 60, 65; Spreadthesign iv, 16, 21, 31, 45, 60, 65; Lauren Murray 81bc, 82bc

All other images © Pearson Education Limited

Notes from the publisher
Pearson has robust editorial processes, including answer and fact checks, to ensure the accuracy of the content in this publication, and every effort is made to ensure this publication is free of errors. We are, however, only human, and occasionally errors do occur. Pearson is not liable for any misunderstandings that arise as a result of errors in this publication, but it is our priority to ensure that the content is accurate. If you spot an error, please do contact us at resourcescorrections@pearson.com so we can make sure it is corrected.

Contents

About this book

This book will help your child to improve their basic literacy skills, fill gaps in learning and increase confidence in a fun and engaging way. It offers a simple, approachable way for you to guide your child through the grammar and punctuation requirements of the National Curriculum.

Your child's mastery of grammar will allow them to express themselves clearly and meet expectations within the whole English curriculum, and beyond!

Grammar and punctuation made clear

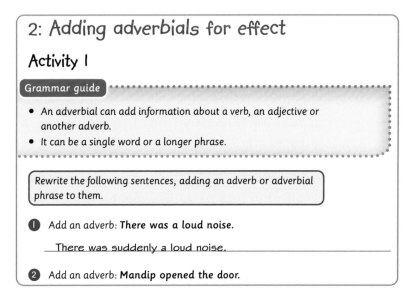

- This activity book is split into bite-sized, manageable topics that are clearly named.
- Each topic is broken down into a number of sessions that develop particular skills and understanding.
- Every session includes grammar or punctuation guides, which give 'at a glance' guidance.

- Then three activities introduce, practise and reinforce the skill focus.
- Completing all three activities in one sitting will help your child get to grips with the concept.
- There are checkpoints for your child to fill in at the end of each topic. This gives you the chance to see where further support is needed.

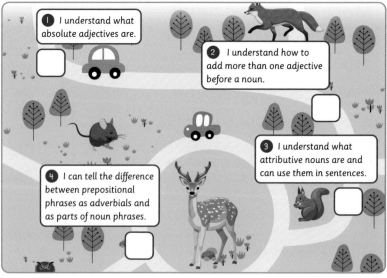

- Short sessions work best. Try setting aside half an hour for your child to explore the three activities.

- Try to complete the topics in the given order, as many of them form key foundations for the ones that follow.

- Your child will ideally work through topics independently, but it's worth being there for when support is needed.

- If your child seems bored or is struggling, suggest they take a break. It might be that they understand the ideas already, or just need time to take something in. They could work on a creative task, such as colouring or following patterns. Try the Pearson Handwriting Activity Workbooks: they contain lots of fun activities, and will also help your child to practise pencil control.

- At the end of a topic, explore the checkpoints with your child and make sure you're happy with what they've understood.

Building from ...

These topics follow on directly from Year 3 to Year 4:

Year 3 topic	Year 4 topic
Adverbials	Fronted adverbials
Demonstratives	Revising determiners and pronouns
Possession	Understanding 's'
Prepositions	More expanded noun phrases
More conjunctions	Conjunctions and prepositions for effect
Verb forms	Verb forms for Standard English
Direct speech	Punctuation

Building towards ...

These topics follow on directly from Year 4 to Year 5:

Year 4 topic	Year 5 topic
Revising determiners and pronouns	Demonstratives
Verb forms for Standard English	Verb forms
More expanded noun phrases	Relative clauses
Fronted adverbials	Exploring adverbials
Punctuation	Punctuation

Getting started

- Make your child's learning space interesting and fun, in a favourite place to sit or with a favourite toy beside them.
- Encourage your child to step away from any technology or energetic games a little while beforehand, and to take some deep breaths to help them focus.
- Make sure they're sitting comfortably at a table and holding their pencil properly.
- Try to sit with your child to start, even if you're occupied with your own task.

A helping hand

Remind your child to ask for help when they need it. In some topics, you may find they need a little extra guidance. Follow the tips below to support them.

As in Year 3, children will benefit from considering and saying sentences before writing them. Try to take some time to listen to these: an audience could help your child to clarify their ideas.

Grammar guide

"These are for all of *you*," said Peeta. "*You* deserve *them*!"
He had made cakes for *us*, and *they* looked delicious! I thanked *him* and handed *them* to you. You gave one back to *me* and passed two to *her*. She handed one back, and *we* shared it. It tasted like honey.

- Pronouns are words that stand in for nouns, including names.
- Personal pronouns represent the 'first person', 'second person' or 'third person'. They can be **singular** or *plural*.
- The subject of a sentence is the person or thing doing the action.
- The <u>subject personal pronouns</u> are 'I', 'you' singular, 'he', 'she', 'it', 'we', 'you' plural and 'they'.
- The object of a sentence is not doing the action, but is involved in the action.
- The <u>object personal pronouns</u> are 'me', 'you' singular, 'him', 'her', 'it', 'us', 'you' plural and 'them'.

"In my opinion," said Tom, "you're wrong."

- Some sentences tell us someone's speech. The speech goes inside speech marks. These are also called inverted commas because they look like upside-down commas.
- Speech punctuation changes when the identifier comes in the middle of the speech. If this happens, it should be at a natural break in the sentence.
- The first part of a speech sentence still starts with an capital letter, but the identifier and the second part of the speech sentence do not.
- The first part of a speech sentence ends with a comma inside the speech marks.
- The identifier also ends with a comma.
- The second part of the speech sentence ends with its full stop, question mark or exclamation mark inside the speech marks.

Activity 3

Write short sentences on these topics. Use a different kind of adverbial in each, and label it to show what kind of information it adds.

❶ Describe something that happened during a sport or game.

_____

❷ Explain a decision you have made.

Determiners and pronouns (pages 2–16)

This topic includes a swift recap of learning from previous years. If your child struggles with any aspect of this, it may help for them to look back at their previous work.

Punctuation: Another way to write speech (pages 56–57) and Punctuating dialogue (pages 58–59)

The rules for punctuating speech can seem hard. Working closely through the grammar guides will help, and you could find other examples for your child to study next to the rules. At times, your child may also need help revising rules from earlier activities.

Tricky concepts

Adverbials and prepositional phrases

Adverbials and prepositional phrases can give information about things such as time (e.g. 'after lunch'), place (e.g. 'at home') or cause (e.g. 'for Mum'). Encourage your child to look closely at the examples on pages 32, 34 and 41.

Determiners and pronouns

Some words can be determiners or pronouns depending on their context (such as 'I like that hat.' / 'I like that.'). However, some can be both at the same time. Possessive determiners such as 'her' in 'her hat' are still pronouns because they stand in for possessive nouns (such as 'Anbara's hat').

Technical terms

Even when children know and understand the structures of grammar, terminology can make things seem difficult. Help your child to use the Glossary, which makes the terms clearer.

Progress check

- Once your child has worked on some activities, judge how confident they are with carrying on alone. If they're keen for independence, they're probably on the right track.
- Encourage your child to talk to you about what they are learning. Getting an explanation in their own words will show you how much they've understood.

Extension activities

- Challenge your child to investigate the fronted adverbials they spot while reading. They should consider what kind of information each gives (such as details about number or manner), and also whether it contains a preposition or a conjunction.
- It is difficult to explore cohesion and paragraph structure in short activities, so challenge your child to develop their understanding in longer pieces of writing. Suggest projects that will interest them, such as creating an information text about a favourite hobby.

Putting grammar and punctuation skills to use

Help your child to understand that their new grammar and punctuation skills are in use everywhere. Encourage them to find examples around them, including in their reading materials.

- To progress from Year 3's focus on non-fiction structure, ask your child to look at paragraph flow and cohesion in traditional tales and myths.
- When your child is asked to include dialogue in composition activities, encourage them to check their accuracy by looking back at the grammar guides in this Activity Book.

Determiners and pronouns

1: Simple determiners

Activity 1

> ### Grammar guide
>
> I'd like <u>some</u> <u>breakfast</u>. Please pass <u>a piece of</u> <u>toast</u> and <u>the</u> jam.
> I don't want <u>any</u> <u>cereal</u> but I'd like <u>all of the</u> strawberries.
>
> - **Determiners** go before both simple and expanded <u>noun phrases</u>.
> - They can be single words or phrases.
> - They tell us whether something is singular or plural and definite or indefinite.
> - **Indefinite determiners** indicate a general type of thing: something not specific.
> - **Definite determiners** indicate something known and specific.

> Underline the definite determiners.
> Circle the indefinite determiners.

He peered around. Some of the doors would have alarms, and <u>each</u> window was locked. A few windows would have alarms, too. Perhaps he could escape through that skylight, at the end of one corridor he'd seen. A jump from the roof might be possible.

Activity 2

Grammar guide

> I enjoy **no** sports. I enjoy **a few** sports. I enjoy **all** sports.
> Dido ate **a** pizza. Dido ate **some** pizza. Dido ate **every** pizza.

- **Quantitative determiners** give information about quantity.
- They can help to make meaning clear and accurate.
- In the examples above, the different determiners create very different meanings.

> Write down the determiners that you found in Activity 1.
> Make notes about the information they give about number.

<u>Some of the: There's more than one door but not all have alarms.</u>

_____

_____

_____

_____

Activity 3

> Say this story aloud, adding different quantitative determiners.
> Write the ones you think are best in the gaps.

We had _____ knowledge of where we were.

Somehow, we'd got lost and ended up in _____ forest.

We had _____ water left, and _____ food.

There were now _____ ways for us to get home.

2: Personal pronouns

Activity 1

Grammar guide

"These are for all of *you*," said Peeta. "*You* deserve *them*!"
He had made cakes for *us*, and *they* looked delicious! **I** thanked **him** and handed *them* to **you**. **You** gave one back to **me** and passed two to **her**. **She** handed one back, and *we* shared it. **It** tasted like honey.

- Pronouns are words that stand in for nouns, including names.
- Personal pronouns represent the 'first person', 'second person' or 'third person'. They can be **singular** or *plural*.
- The subject of a sentence is the person or thing doing the action.
- The subject personal pronouns are 'I', 'you' singular, 'he', 'she', 'it', 'we', 'you' plural and 'they'.
- The object of a sentence is not doing the action, but is involved in the action.
- The object personal pronouns are 'me', 'you' singular, 'him', 'her', 'it', 'us', 'you' plural and 'them'.

Use the information in the grammar guide to add pronouns and complete the table.

		Subject pronouns			Object pronouns		
Singular	1st person						
	2nd person						
	3rd person						
Plural	1st person						
	2nd person						
	3rd person						

Activity 2

Look at the coloured nouns and pronouns. Circle the ones that you would choose to use. Think about grammar, repetition and meaning. It may help if you read the paragraph aloud.

My sister and (I) / me had been waiting for ages for the train / it to arrive. The train / It finally screeched to a stop and our father stepped off the train / it. Our father / He / Him waved and smiled at my sister and me / we / us with such joy that my father / he / him dropped the suitcases. The suitcases / They / Them fell with a thud, but my father, my sister and I / we / us were so happy to see each other that none of my father, my sister and I / we / us cared.

Activity 3

In each pair of sentences, circle the pronoun and underline the noun phrase it represents.

1. The girl hurried up the steps.
   Suddenly, she tripped and fell.

2. The sound of the crowd filled the stadium.
   It could be heard even from the car park.

3. My brother ordered a burger.
   The waiter smiled down at him.

3: Demonstrative determiners

Activity 1

Grammar guide

> I got **these** posters for **this** wall, and **those** posters for **that** wall.

- The four demonstratives are 'this', 'that', 'these' and 'those'.
  - The demonstratives '**this**' and '**that**' indicate singular nouns.
  - The demonstratives '**these**' and '**those**' indicate plural nouns.
  - The demonstratives '**this**' and '**these**' indicate items that are nearby.
  - The demonstratives '**that**' and '**those**' indicate items further away.
- The demonstratives can be used as determiners.

Underline the demonstrative determiner in each sentence.

Tick the boxes to show whether it indicates something 'indefinite' or 'definite', 'singular' or 'plural' and 'near' or 'far'.

1. Did you hear <u>that</u> thunder?
   - ☐ indefinite ☑ singular ☐ near
   - ☑ definite ☐ plural ☑ far

2. This quiz is the hardest we've had.
   - ☐ indefinite ☐ singular ☐ near
   - ☐ definite ☐ plural ☐ far

3. Would you like any help with those bags?
   - ☐ indefinite ☐ singular ☐ near
   - ☐ definite ☐ plural ☐ far

4. These wasps just won't leave us alone!
   - ☐ indefinite ☐ singular ☐ near
   - ☐ definite ☐ plural ☐ far

Activity 2

1 Identify which demonstrative determiner would be appropriate before each subject.

a the pen in my hand   _____this_____ pen

b next door's roses   _____ roses

c the crackers I'm eating   _____ crackers

d the idea you had yesterday _____ idea

2 Add the correct demonstrative determiner to each of the following sentences.

a We're so high up that _____ people look like tiny ants.

b You should borrow _____ book I'm reading – it's fantastic.

c _____ song you sang in last week's concert was beautiful.

d Come and look at _____ plans for the new school playground.

Activity 3

Use each demonstrative determiner to begin a noun phrase about something you can see.

1 _____

2 _____

3 _____

4 _____

4: Demonstrative pronouns

Activity 1

- The demonstratives 'this', 'that', 'these' and 'those' can also be pronouns.
- They stand in for nouns or noun phrases, and indicate whether things are singular or plural and near or far.

> Identify which demonstrative pronoun would be appropriate to complete each sentence.

1 I usually can't find any seashells, but today I've collected all __these__ !

2 We need the wide paintbrushes – have you seen any of _____?

3 Do you not have a ruler? You can use _____, after I've finished with it.

4 I used to enjoy judo, but I don't do _____ any more.

Activity 2

We started **running**, in an attempt to catch up. Even **that** wasn't enough.

- The demonstratives '**that**' and '**this**' can represent more than just noun phrases.
- They can also represent, for example, **actions**, ideas or sequences of events.
- This helps to create links between sentences.

1 Underline the demonstrative pronoun in each paragraph. Note briefly what it indicates.

a We decided to get flowers and take them to Gran in the hospital. We hoped <u>that</u> would cheer her up.

getting flowers _____

_____

b It's Monday, so I head to the sports centre for my karate lesson. This is always the best part of my week.

_____

_____

c My uncle keeps telling me, 'Good things come to those who wait.' That's a nice idea – but I'm not certain it's true.

_____

_____

2 Write the demonstrative pronoun that could replace each underlined phrase.

a When she left the room, I tasted the curry Mary had been cooking. "<u>The curry you have been cooking</u> is delicious!" I called.

_____

b On my ninth birthday, I tripped and landed face first in my cake. <u>My ninth birthday</u> was the most embarrassing day of my life.

_____

Activity 3

Write a sentence describing an opinion you have heard. Start a second one with 'This' or 'That' and explain why you agree or disagree with the opinion.

_____

_____

_____

5: Possessive determiners

Activity 1

Grammar guide

> Their stories are similar, but our stories aren't. My tale is about a spy, and your story is scary. Her story is set in a jungle. His tale is funny, but its ending is sad.

- **Possessive pronouns** represent possessive nouns.
- They show that something belongs to someone or something else. This could mean it is owned by them or is related to them in a different way.
- Some possessive pronouns are **determiners**. These are: 'my', 'your' singular, 'his', 'her', 'its', 'our', 'your' plural and 'their'. They are called **possessive determiners**.

Add possessive determiners to these sentences.
Use each determiner once.

1. Karen and I were delighted that __our__ project had worked so well.

2. The villain turned to me, cackled in _____ face and twirled _____ moustache wickedly.

3. You stood up, straightened _____ tie and followed Miss Smith into _____ office.

4. Most of the geese stretched _____ wings and took off, but one stayed on _____ nest.

Activity 2

> Look at the underlined words in each sentence. Change them to a noun phrase that includes a possessive determiner.

1. It may be hard to change <u>the opinions of these people</u>.

   <u>their opinions</u>

2. This is a new subject, but <u>the basic ideas of the subject</u> will be familiar.

   _____

3. Genie and I are going to meet <u>the friends we have</u> after class.

   _____

4. Please would you tidy <u>the desk where you are working</u>?

   _____

Activity 3

> Write three sentences about things done by you and your family or friends. Use a different possessive determiner in each sentence.

_____

_____

_____

_____

_____

6: Independent possessive pronouns

Activity 1

> In the story contest, **ours** were all considered. **Yours** won because its characters were the best. **Mine** came second and **his** came third. **Hers** and **theirs** were runners up.

- **Independent possessive pronouns** represent both the owner and the thing owned.
- The words 'mine', 'yours' singular, 'his', 'hers', 'its', 'ours', 'yours' plural and 'theirs' are independent possessive pronouns.

Write the meaning of each independent possessive pronoun in the following passage.

Velma and the twins worked on their models. Hers was ready but theirs wasn't yet.

"How's yours coming along?" Velma asked one of the twins. Jo sighed. "The idea for ours was originally mine, although Vicente said it was his. It doesn't really matter, though – we're working as a team now!"

Independent possessive pronouns	Meanings
hers	Velma's model

Activity 2

Use independent possessive pronouns to replace the repetitive noun phrases.

1. We hung our paintings, but their paintings aren't dry yet.

   <u>We hung our paintings, but theirs aren't dry yet.</u>

2. I've lost my book. Can I borrow your book?

3. Your lunch looks tastier than our lunch.

4. She drank her tea, but his tea was too hot.

Activity 3

Use the possessive pronoun 'mine' to write a sentence of your own.

7: Creating clarity and cohesion

Activity 1

Grammar guide

- Determiners can give different kinds of basic information. This can be about number, whether something is definite, position, who owns it or where it comes from.
- Determiners should be used accurately to make meaning clear.

Imagine you are looking at a boy who is holding seven cards. Complete the following sentences with three different accurate determiners:

- one quantitative determiner other than 'seven'
- one demonstrative determiner
- one possessive determiner.

1 I can see _____ cards.

2 I can see _____ cards.

3 I can see _____ cards.

Activity 2

Grammar guide

- If a paragraph has cohesion, the sentences in it are linked together to become effective as a whole.
- Pronouns can create cohesion by referring back to nouns that come before them.

Write a cohesive paragraph about a day at school, using at least **three** of the following kinds of pronoun to avoid repetition.

- subject personal
- object personal
- possessive
- demonstrative
- relative

_____

_____

_____

_____

_____

_____

Activity 3

Look back at the sentences you wrote in Activity 2. Mark any of your pronouns that remove clarity. Mark where you could use any more pronouns without losing clarity.

What do I Know?

1 I can identify and use definite and indefinite determiners.

2 I can identify and use all the subject and object personal pronouns.

3 I can identify and use all four demonstrative determiners.

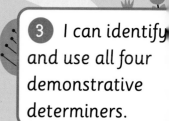

5 I understand that the demonstrative pronouns 'this' and 'that' can also represent actions, ideas or sequences of events.

4 I understand and can use 'this', 'that', 'these' and 'those'.

6 I can identify and use the possessive pronouns that are used as determiners.

7 I can identify and use the independent possessive pronouns.

9 I can use different kinds of pronouns to avoid repetition and create cohesion in my writing.

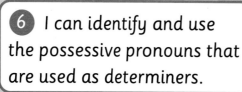

8 I can select different kinds of determiners to make meaning clear.

1: What do you remember about verb forms?

Activity 1

> Today, I meet Shaurya. **She works** in town.
> The shops **are** nearby.
>
> Last month, I met Shaurya. **She worked** in town.
> The shops **were** nearby.

- Standard English is just English with the right spelling, grammar and punctuation.
- Using the correct **verb forms** is vital for Standard English.
- Verbs must agree with the **subject** and **tense** of their sentence. This means they must have changed correctly to show **who or what does the action** and **when the action happens**.

Circle the verbs in this paragraph that are not in Standard English.

We (is) nervous because I is about to meet my friend's parents. It's my friend's birthday, so they says we could all going out for pizza. I done not eat meat so I hope the pizza place had some good vegetarian toppings. Sometimes restaurants forgot about them.

Activity 2

Grammar guide

> I <u>had seen</u> a hawk flying over the field. We <u>were hoping</u> to see it again.
> I <u>have seen</u> a hawk flying over the field. We <u>are hoping</u> to see it again.

- **Perfect verbs** show that actions are perfectly complete. This could be in the <u>past</u> or in the <u>present</u>.
- They are formed with the auxiliary verb 'to have' and a past participle.
- The past participle is usually the same as a verb's past tense.
- **Progressive verbs** show that something continues over a period of time. This could be in the <u>past</u> or in the <u>present</u>, too.
- They are formed with the auxiliary verb 'to be' and a present participle.
- The past participle is a verb ending '–ing'.

Circle the auxiliary verbs and underline the participles. Then write what tense each sentence is in: present perfect, past perfect, present progressive or past progressive.

1. I (have) <u>hurried</u> home.   <u>present perfect</u>

2. I was hurrying home.   _____

3. I am hurrying home.   _____

4. I had hurried home.   _____

Activity 3

Tick the sentences with correctly formed verbs. Circle the mistakes in the others.

- Where have you been?   ☐
- The days are getting shorter.   ☐
- I have has enough to eat.   ☐
- They were getting fed up.   ☐

- We has started already.   ☐
- Nami had heard the story.   ☐
- Anika were planning a party.   ☐
- These chores are took ages.   ☐

2: Creating Standard English

Activity 1

Grammar guide

- Standard English is just English with the right spelling, grammar and punctuation.
- Using the correct verb forms is vital for Standard English.
- Verbs must agree with the subject and tense of their sentence. This means they must have changed correctly to show who or what does the action and when the action happens.

Look again at this paragraph from the previous lesson, where you identified the incorrect verbs. Rewrite the verbs to show what the correct ones would be.

I is nervous because I is about to meet my friend's parents. It's my friend's birthday, so they says we could all going out for pizza. I done not eat meat so I hope the pizza place had some good vegetarian toppings. Sometimes restaurants forgot about them.

① __am__   ② _____   ③ _____   ④ _____

⑤ _____   ⑥ _____   ⑦ _____

Activity 2

Grammar guide

- Perfect verbs show that actions are perfectly complete. This could be in the past or in the present.
- Progressive verbs show that something continues over a period of time. This could be in the past or in the present, too.

1 To answer the questions below, give the correct verb form rather than just the infinitive verb.

a What auxiliary verb is used in the past perfect tense? _____

b What auxiliary verbs can be used in the present perfect tense? _____

c What auxiliary verbs can be used in the past progressive tense? _____

d What auxiliary verbs can be used in the past perfect tense? _____

2 Tick one box to show what kind of participle should be used for each type of verb. Write one example of each.

Type of verb	Kind of participle		Example
Progressive verbs	Present participle	◯	
	Past participle	◯	
Perfect verbs	Present participle	◯	
	Past participle	◯	

Activity 3

Rewrite this paragraph, correcting the verbs so it becomes Standard English.

My cousin Yael are training as a dancer. He go to a ballet school. Before he apply, he had practising every day. Now the practice had worked: he is lived his dream. We was hoping to watch him perform last week.

_____

_____

_____

_____

What do I Know?

1 I know that, in Standard English, verb forms have to agree with their subject and tense.

2 I remember how perfect and progressive verbs are formed.

3 I can form perfect and progressive verbs.

4 I can correct verbs to create Standard English.

More expanded noun phrases

1: Exploring adjectives

Activity 1

Grammar guide

> I saw a **very big, strong** tree. It had **impressively long, thin, leafy** branches.

- There are lots of ways to expand noun phrases. Using **adjectives** is one of them.
- **Adverbials** can be used to give more information to adjectives.
- There could be more than one **adjective** before a **noun**.
- These **adjectives** are usually separated by **commas**, like items in a list.

1 Underline every adjective in the following sentences.

> Our neighbours have a <u>friendly</u> dog. It has a loud, booming bark. We sometimes go on long, refreshing walks in the country with them, and we see the dog having a great time.

2 Rewrite this sentence, adding two adjectives before each noun and separating them with commas.

They were going on a journey to the mountains.

_____

_____

Activity 2

Grammar guide

> Most were wide, healthy **green** leaves, but some were dry **dead** ones.

- Some adjectives are called **absolute adjectives**.
- An absolute adjective is one that could not have adverbials of degree such as 'very' or 'a bit' before it.
- For example, nothing could be just a bit dead. Something could not be a bit black, or it would be grey. All colours are counted as absolute adjectives.
- In a group of adjectives, do not use a comma before an absolute adjective.
- Any absolute adjectives come at the end of the group, just before the noun.

Tick one box to show which version of each sentence is correct.

1 The farmer cared for the fluffy white lambs. ✓

The farmer cared for the fluffy, white lambs. ☐

2 Under the bridge, Sala saw a big, slimy smelly troll. ☐

Under the bridge, Sala saw a big, slimy, smelly troll. ☐

3 We tried to take a photo of the green stunning bird. ☐

We tried to take a photo of the stunning green bird. ☐

4 It was a completely, unexpected, utterly, astonishing sight. ☐

It was a completely unexpected, utterly astonishing sight. ☐

5 There was a clear, blue sky overhead. ☐

There was a clear blue sky overhead. ☐

Activity 3

Rewrite the sentence, adding all of the adjectives below.

purple   quick   strange

final   desperate

The creature made one attempt to escape.

_____

_____

_____

_____

2: Adding extra nouns

Activity 1

Grammar guide

> We played in the **village park**, which is near the **bus stop**.

- Some words that give detail to **nouns** are **other nouns**. They are called **attributive nouns**.
- They do not describe what something is **like**, like adjectives do. They can show what kind of thing it is, what it is for, where it is, what it is made from or many other details.

Underline the attributive nouns in these sentences.

Our last <u>family</u> trip was to the beach. I remember there was an ice-cream van parked by the sea wall, and that I helped my young cousin to build sand castles.

Activity 2

Tick one box by each sentence to show whether the underlined word is an adjective or attributive noun.

1. That's a <u>toy</u> car. ☐ Adjective ☑ Attributive noun
2. That's a <u>red</u> car. ☐ Adjective ☐ Attributive noun
3. That's an <u>old</u> car. ☐ Adjective ☐ Attributive noun
4. That's a <u>family</u> car. ☐ Adjective ☐ Attributive noun

Activity 3

> Add these nouns as attributive nouns to the sentences.
> Use each only once.

car	school	tennis	music

I was meant to meet my mum by the _____ gates

so she could drop off my _____ racket. Before I

got there, though, I saw her in the _____ park

chatting to my _____ teacher.

3: Exploring prepositional phrases

Activity 1

Grammar guide

> The clock on the wall chimed at 9 o'clock.

- **Prepositional phrases** can be used to expand <u>noun phrases</u>. They are parts of noun phrases if they add detail about a **noun**.
- **Prepositional phrases** can also be <u>adverbial phrases</u>. They are adverbials if they add information about a **verb**, or about the whole of the sentence.

> Tick a box to show how each prepositional phrase is used.

1 Gita ate <u>at the canteen</u>.

- ☑ Adverbial
- ☐ Part of a noun phrase

2 The tree <u>in the garden</u> grows apples.

- ☐ Adverbial
- ☐ Part of a noun phrase

3 I handed in my homework <u>for maths class</u>.

- ☐ Adverbial
- ☐ Part of a noun phrase

4 We searched <u>around the whole house</u>.

- ☐ Adverbial
- ☐ Part of a noun phrase

Activity 2

Grammar guide

Prepositional phrases can add information about different things when they are in noun phrases, as well as when they are adverbials. For example:
- time (for example, the bus <u>at noon</u>)
- cause (for example, the fundraiser <u>in aid of charity</u>)
- place (for example, the house <u>on the hill</u>)
- quality (for example, the man <u>with curly hair</u>).

Draw lines to match each sentence to the kind of information its prepositional phrase adds.

1. The journey to reach the river was quicker than it seemed.

2. Mika's return at 10 o'clock was too late for supper.

3. The firefighter was awarded a glistening medal of solid gold.

4. It was a weary, dusty walk along the road, but we did it.

quality

time

place

cause

Activity 3

1. Expand the noun phrase in this sentence with a prepositional phrase showing **place**. This will add information about where the bridge is.

We crossed the bridge _over a river_ .

2. Expand the noun phrase in this sentence with a prepositional phrase showing **quality**. This will add information about what the house is like.

We saw a house _____ .

3. Expand the noun phrase in this sentence with a prepositional phrase showing **time**. This will add information about when the meeting is.

We're going to miss the meeting _____ .

4: Expanding noun phrases

Activity 1

Grammar guide

I wrote a <u>long experiment report for science class</u>.

- There are lots of ways to expand <u>noun phrases</u>. They all add extra information to a **noun**.
- A noun phrase could be expanded using an **adjective**, an **attributive noun** or a **prepositional phrase** – or more than one of these things.

Tick at least one box by each sentence to show how the underlined noun phrase has been expanded. You may need to tick more than one box for some sentences.

1. Suki had broken <u>her gym bag</u>.
   - ☐ Adjective
   - ☑ Attributive noun
   - ☐ Prepositional phrase

2. Now she needed <u>a good bag with a strong handle</u>.
   - ☐ Adjective
   - ☐ Attributive noun
   - ☐ Prepositional phrase

3. <u>A friendly shop assistant</u> helped her to find one.
   - ☐ Adjective
   - ☐ Attributive noun
   - ☐ Prepositional phrase

4. It was on <u>a shelf at the very back of the shop</u>.
   - ☐ Adjective
   - ☐ Attributive noun
   - ☐ Prepositional phrase

Activity 2

> Expand each noun phrase using an adjective, an attributive noun or a prepositional phrase. Use each of these things only once.

1 the homework

_____

2 my bike

_____

3 his collection

_____

Activity 3

> Write sentences of your own that include expanded noun phrases. Use at least one adjective, at least one attributive noun and at least one prepositional phrase to expand the noun phrases.

_____

_____

_____

_____

_____

_____

What do I Know?

1. I understand what absolute adjectives are.

2. I understand how to add more than one adjective before a noun.

3. I understand what attributive nouns are and can use them in sentences.

4. I can tell the difference between prepositional phrases as adverbials and as parts of noun phrases.

5. I understand how prepositional phrases can add different kinds of information.

6. I can use adjectives, prepositional phrases and attributive nouns to expand noun phrases.

31

Fronted adverbials

1: Exploring adverbials

Activity 1

> Kelly **quickly kicked** the ball <u>**with all her strength**</u>.
> She was **just** so **pleased** when she scored a goal.

- An adverbial could be a **single word** or a **longer phrase**.
- An adverbial can add information about a **verb**, **adjective** or another **adverb**.
- <u>Prepositional phrases</u> can be adverbials, if they add information about a verb, an adjective or another adverb rather than a noun.

> Underline the adverbials in these sentences. Tick the one that uses a prepositional phrase as the adverbial.

1 He closed his eyes and loudly began to snore. ☐

2 The maths lesson began at 11 o'clock. ☐

3 I often try eating new foods. ☐

4 I play ball only outside. ☐

Activity 2

> It was **extremely** hot **that day**.

Like prepositional phrases in noun phrases, all adverbials can add information about any of the following things.

- **time** (such as 'this morning')
- **cause** (such as 'to help my mum')
- **place** (such as 'at home')
- **number** (such as 'twice')
- **manner** (such as 'happily')
- **probability** (such as 'maybe')
- **degree** (such as 'very')
- **frequency** (such as 'once a day')

1 Draw lines to show what kind of information the adverbial adds to each sentence.

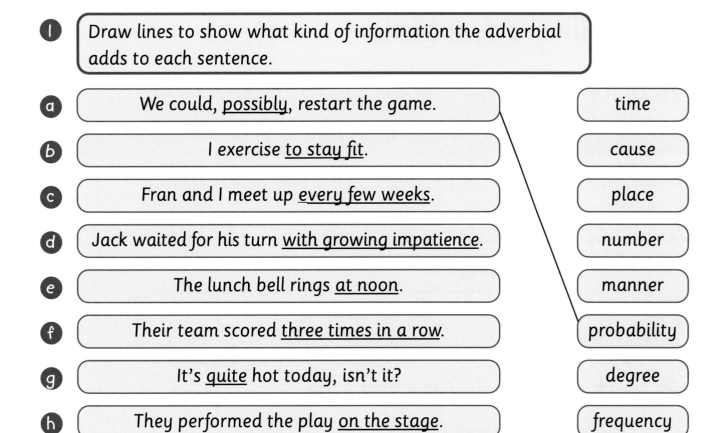

a We could, <u>possibly</u>, restart the game.

b I exercise <u>to stay fit</u>.

c Fran and I meet up <u>every few weeks</u>.

d Jack waited for his turn <u>with growing impatience</u>.

e The lunch bell rings <u>at noon</u>.

f Their team scored <u>three times in a row</u>.

g It's <u>quite</u> hot today, isn't it?

h They performed the play <u>on the stage</u>.

time

cause

place

number

manner

probability

degree

frequency

2 Look again at the sentences in Question 1. Which sentences use prepositional phrases as their adverbials? Write their letters here.

Activity 3

Underline the adverbials in the story, and then read the story without them. Check that each sentence still makes sense.

Controlling her fear, Sofi slowly opened the door. It creaked as it swung away. She could see a few stairs in front of her. She descended into the blackness. Every now and again, there was a soft noise from below her. Sofi hesitated only once. She wanted to solve the mystery so she could finally go home.

2: Adding adverbials for effect

Activity 1

- An adverbial can add information about a verb, an adjective or another adverb.
- It can be a single word or a longer phrase.

Rewrite the following sentences, adding an adverb or adverbial phrase to them.

1 Add an adverb: **There was a loud noise.**

There was suddenly a loud noise.

2 Add an adverb: **Mandip opened the door.**

_____

3 Add an adverbial phrase: **We had a science lesson.**

_____

Activity 2

Adverbials can add information about any of the following things.

- time (such as 'yesterday')'
- cause (such as 'for our holiday')'
- place (such as 'in the garden')
- number (such as 'three times')
- manner (such as 'with a smile')
- probability (such as 'perhaps')
- degree (such as 'completely')
- frequency (such as 'weekly')

Rewrite the following sentences, adding an adverbial to each one.

1 Add an adverbial of **manner** to show how something happens.

The dish fell.

_____ The dish fell with a clatter. _____

2 Add an adverbial of **probability** to show how likely it is that something will happen.

We'll arrive by noon.

_____

3 Add an adverbial of **frequency** to show how often something happens.

I travel by train.

_____

4 Add an adverbial of **degree** to show how extreme a description is.

I am pleased to see you.

_____

Activity 3

Write short sentences on these topics. Use a different kind of adverbial in each, and label it to show what kind of information it adds.

1 Describe something that happened during a sport or game.

_____

2 Explain a decision you have made.

_____

3: What are fronted adverbials?

Activity 1

Grammar guide

With a crash, the plate fell to the floor.

- A *fronted adverbial* is an adverbial that is placed at the start of a sentence.
- It is always followed by a **comma**.

Tick the sentences that include fronted adverbials.

- After finishing our exams, my friends and I went camping. ☑
- As the sun rose, the birds began to sing. ☐
- She answered immediately, without a second thought. ☐
- With surprise, I wondered how he could have run so quickly. ☐
- Tell me, do you know where we are? ☐

Activity 2

1 | Out loud, read each pair of instruction sentences. Write notes about why a fronted adverbial might be chosen for each.

a Nod your head after counting to ten.
After counting to ten, nod your head.

<u>We need to know not to nod straight away.</u>

b Put in the eggs without breaking their yolks.
Without breaking their yolks, put in the eggs.

_____

2 | In your head, read each pair of story sentences. Write notes about why a fronted adverbial might be chosen for each.

a There was suddenly a crash.
Suddenly, there was a crash.

_____

b There was a mysterious noise from deep within the undergrowth.
From deep within the undergrowth, there was a mysterious noise.

_____

Activity 3

In one or more sentences, explain why writers may choose to use fronted adverbials.

_____

_____

_____

4: Conjunctions in fronted adverbials

Activity 1

Grammar guide

> We couldn't play outside **because it was raining**.
> **Because it was raining**, we couldn't play outside.

- A **subordinate clause**, with its **subordinating conjunction**, can be used as a fronted adverbial.
- Clauses haven't been swapped in position around the conjunction, like two main clauses can be.
- Instead, the conjunction moves to the start of the sentence with the subordinate clause.

Tick the sentences that correctly use subordinate clauses as fronted adverbials.

- When the clock struck twelve, she hurried home. ☑

- If you promise to return it, you can use my coat. ☐

- I really want to see you, I'm not free today although. ☐

- So I didn't ruin the surprise, I closed my eyes tightly. ☐

- And he didn't trip over, Suni turned on his torch. ☐

- When the sun rose Chloë woke up. ☐

Activity 2

1 Write two sentences made up of a main clause, a subordinating conjunction and then a subordinate clause.

a _____

_____

b _____

_____

2 Rewrite your sentences, using the conjunctions and subordinate clauses as fronted adverbials.

a _____

_____

b _____

_____

Activity 3

Look back at Activity 1. Rewrite the sentences that you did **not** tick, correcting the mistakes.

_____

_____

_____

_____

5: Adding fronted adverbials

Activity 1

Grammar guide

A fronted adverbial comes at the start of a sentence, followed by a comma.

1 Rewrite each sentence, moving the underlined words to the start of the sentence. Remember to add a comma.

a There was a reaction <u>immediately</u>.

  Immediately, there was a reaction.

b She ran all the way home <u>so she wasn't late</u>.

_____

c I saw, <u>in the mirror</u>, someone else.

_____

2 Which of the sentences above uses a preposition to begin its fronted adverbial? Which uses a subordinating conjunction? Write their letters.

a Preposition: _____

b Subordinating conjunction: _____

Activity 2

Grammar guide

Adverbials can add information about any of the following things.

- time (such as 'at 12 o'clock')
- cause (such as 'due to snow')
- place (such as 'in town')
- number (such as 'firstly')

- manner (such as 'quickly')
- probability (such as 'possibly')
- degree (such as 'a bit')
- frequency (such as 'every month')

Add the right kind of fronted adverbial to each sentence. Try to include one adverbial that starts with a preposition, and one that starts with a subordinating conjunction.

1. Add a fronted adverbial of **time** to show when something happens.

   I saw my friends.

   Yesterday, I saw my friends.

2. Add a fronted adverbial of **place** to show where something happens.

   I was playing rounders.

   _____

3. Add a fronted adverbial of **cause** to show why something happens.

   I cleaned my room.

   _____

4. Add a fronted adverbial of **number** to how many times something has happened.

   I found a four-leaf clover.

   _____

Activity 3

Use a fronted adverbial to write a gripping first sentence for a mystery story about a hidden room.

_____

_____

_____

_____

_____

6: Forming topical paragraphs

Activity 1

In my spare time, I like to skateboard. My sister's been teaching me, and I'm definitely getting better. I also like to go to the park to meet my friends.

- A paragraph is a group of sentences about the same topic. Dividing writing into paragraphs can make it easier to read.
- If a fronted adverbial comes at the start of the first sentence in a paragraph, it can help to signal a topic for the whole paragraph. It can act a bit like a sub-heading.
- In a piece of writing, a new paragraph is usually needed when the topic, time or setting changes.

Read the information text below.

The Roman general Julius Caesar invaded Britain over 2,000 years ago, in 55 BCE. He brought a small army and invaded Britain. The tribes living in Britain fought very fiercely, and were much more successful at defending their land than the Romans had expected. The Roman army left, and stayed in France during winter.

In France, Julius Caesar gathered a bigger army. The generals were very skilled in battle techniques and trained the soldiers hard. They got ready to invade Britain again.

The next summer, Caesar and a much bigger army returned to Britain. They were successful enough in battle that the tribes agreed to pay them in return for peace.

For ordinary people, life in Britain changed a lot while the Romans were in charge. The Romans introduced a lot of things we still use now, such as sewers, indoor heating, snack bars and written language.

Look at the information text and write each fronted adverbial in the table. Then write whether it shows a change in topic, time or setting.

Fronted adverbials	Topic, time or setting?

Activity 2

Look at the fronted adverbials below. Write a paragraph of two or three short sentences that suits each topic it introduces.

When I get up in the morning, _____

_____

_____

When I relax in the evening, _____

_____

_____

Activity 3

Write one short paragraph of your own, choosing a suitable fronted adverbial to start it.

_____

_____

_____

What do I know?

1 I can identify the kind of information an adverbial adds to a sentence.

2 I can use adverbials to create specific effects.

3 I understand what fronted adverbials are and what effects they can have.

4 I understand how subordinate clauses can be used as fronted adverbials.

5 I can use fronted adverbials in writing to create special effects.

6 I understand how fronted adverbials can be used to show the topic of a whole paragraph.

45

Punctuation

1: Revising sentence punctuation

Activity 1

This is heavy. Could you come and help me? Hurry up!

- Every sentence starts with an capital letter.
- A statement gives information. It ends in a full stop.
- A question asks for information. It ends with a question mark.
- An exclamation could be cried or shouted suddenly. It could show surprise, pain or strong emotion. It ends with an exclamation mark.

1 Write a statement sentence containing these elements and label it.

verb   capital letter

subject noun   object noun   end punctuation

_____

_____

2 Change your sentence so it becomes a question and label it again. Think about word order and any new words you need, as well as punctuation.

For example: "We can swim."   ➡   "Can we swim?"
"We walk home."   ➡   "Do we walk home?"

_____

_____

Activity 2

Punctuation guide

> Come and get this heavy box. Hurry up!

A command is a **statement** or **exclamation** that gives an instruction.

> Write a short paragraph of a non-fiction text about an animal of your choice. Include at least one statement, one exclamation, one question and one command.

_____

_____

_____

_____

_____

Activity 3

> Look carefully at the punctuation you used in Activity 2. Rewrite any sentences that need correcting.

_____

_____

_____

_____

2: Exploring lists

Activity 1

Punctuation guide

> At the beach, we <u>swam, ate and played</u>.
> At the beach, we <u>swam, ate ice cream and played baseball</u>.

- A <u>list</u> is a series of connected things.
- Most items in a list are separated by **commas**.
- The last two items are connected with '**and**', not separated by a comma.
- If a list is a series of of actions, the **verbs** should all be in the same tense.

1 Follow the example in the Punctuation guide to change these three sentences into one list sentence.

> I hurried home. I got changed. I went to meet my friends.

I hurried home, _____

_____

2 Write a sentence that includes a list of these nouns.

| blackbirds | crows | pigeons | sparrows |

_____

_____

Activity 2

Punctuation guide

> I can hear lots of things from my window: <u>birds, trains, cars and builders</u>.

- You can begin a <u>list</u> sentence using an **introduction** and then a **colon**.
- The **introduction** before a colon should be a full **main clause**.
- A main clause is a group of words including a verb that could stand alone as a sentence.

1 Complete these sentences with punctuation and a list of three actions.

   a This is what I do every day<u>: brush my teeth,</u>_____

         _____

   b In the school holidays, we did lots of activities_____

         _____

2 Add a main clause and a colon as an introduction to this list.

_____ lions, tigers and bears.

Activity 3

Tick the sentences below that contain correctly formed lists.

- We ran, jumped and swim on sports day. ☐
- Sammy watched TV, ate her dinner and went to bed. ☐
- The Smitri family likes to: travel, explore and play tennis. ☐
- I exercise eat healthy food and drink plenty of water to stay fit. ☐
- This is how I learn a spelling: look at it, cover it, write it and check it. ☐

3: Revising possessive apostrophes

Activity 1

Punctuation guide

The bags owned by **Carlos** and the other **pupils** hung near the door of the **classroom**. The coats of younger **children** were there, too.

Carlos's and the other **pupils'** bags hung near the **classroom's** door. Younger **children's** coats were there, too.

- Possession means that something belongs to someone or something else. This could mean it is owned by them or is related to them in a different way.
- A **singular possessive noun** is made up of the noun plus an **apostrophe** and 's'. This includes words that already end '–s'.
- A **plural possessive noun** that ends '–s' takes an **apostrophe** and no extra 's'.
- A **plural noun** that **does not** end '–s' takes an **apostrophe** and 's'.

Tick the sentences that use possessive apostrophes in the correct way.

- A footpath crosses our school's playing field. ⬜
- Peoples' differences are important. ⬜
- The bus's doors opened slowly. ⬜
- Smoke billowed from both of the car's engines. ⬜
- Our trees' leaves were turning golden brown. ⬜
- Lidas friends were waiting for her. ⬜
- The circus' posters are all over town. ⬜
- The women's ideas solved the problem. ⬜

Activity 2

Turn each phrase into a possessive noun phrase.
Then use it in a sentence.

1 the bowl of the dog   <u>the dog's bowl</u>

<u>The dog's bowl is empty.</u>

2 the books of Elias   _____

_____

3 the doors of the houses   _____

_____

4 the wool of the sheep   _____

_____

Activity 3

Look back at Activity 1. Rewrite the sentences you did **not** tick, correcting the mistakes.

_____

_____

_____

_____

_____

4: Exploring contractions

Activity 1

> **Punctuation guide**
>
> | I cannot hear them even though I am listening hard.
> | I can't hear them even though I'm listening hard. |
>
> - **Contractions** are words that have been shortened.
> - **Apostrophes** in contractions show where letters have been missed out.

> Rewrite the sentences below, changing the underlined words to contractions.

> <u>I am</u> annoyed that <u>I cannot</u> see the performances <u>Hallie is</u> in. <u>They are</u> during my holiday. <u>It is</u> such a shame.

I'm annoyed that _____

_____

_____

Activity 2

> **Punctuation guide**
>
> | I **had** longed to meet my hero, but I **have** arrived too late and she **has** left.
> | I'd longed to meet my hero, but I've arrived too late and she's left. |
>
> - Perfect verb forms use the **auxiliary verb** 'to have'.
> - The verb forms 'have', 'has' and 'had' can be **contracted**.

1 Complete the table to show each contraction.

I have arrived.	I've arrived.
He has arrived.	
We have arrived.	
They had arrived.	

2 Rewrite the sentence below, changing the underlined words to contractions.

<u>They had</u> hated the painting <u>I have</u> now displayed, but <u>it has</u> attracted a lot of attention.

_____

_____

_____

Activity 3

Write sentences of your own that include at least four different contractions.

_____

_____

_____

_____

_____

5: Revising direct speech

Activity 1

Punctuation guide

> Rin said, "We're here."   "We're here," **Rin said**.
> She asked, 'Are you there?'   'Are you there?' **she asked**.

- Writing can show speech, which goes inside speech marks. These are also known as inverted commas, because they look like upside-down commas. They can be **double** or **single**, but should stay the same within a piece of writing.
- A new sentence of speech always starts with a **capital letter**.
- When an **identifier** comes before speech:
  - the identifier has a comma after it
  - the punctuation after speech stays as it would usually be, inside the speech marks.
- When an **identifier** comes after speech:
  - the identifier no longer has a capital letter unless it is a proper noun
  - if the speech is a statement, its full stop becomes a comma
  - if the speech is a question or exclamation, the punctuation after it stays as it would usually be, inside the speech marks.

Tick the sentences that use the correct punctuation for speech.

- "Could you clean up?" asked my mum. ☑
- "I was planning to go out." I said. ☐
- Mum replied, "You go out a lot!" ☐
- "I'm helping Kenta with her homework," I cried! ☐
- I said "I'll clean up quickly first." ☐

Activity 2

1 Put each of these sentences into a longer speech sentence, with an identifier at the start.

a It's so beautiful.   Kris said, "It's so beautiful."

b You'd love it here! _____

_____

2 Put each of these sentences into a longer speech sentence, with an identifier at the end.

a I am waiting.   "I am waiting," Ama said.

b Where are you? _____

_____

Activity 3

Look back at Activity 1. Rewrite the sentences you did **not** tick, correcting the mistakes.

_____

_____

_____

6: Another way to write speech

Activity 1

> "In my opinion," said Tom, "you're wrong."

- Some sentences tell us someone's speech. The speech goes inside speech marks. These are also called inverted commas because they look like upside-down commas.
- Speech punctuation changes when the identifier comes in the middle of the speech. If this happens, it should be at a natural break in the sentence.
- The first part of a speech sentence still starts with a capital letter, but the identifier and the second part of the speech sentence do not.
- The first part of a speech sentence ends with a comma inside the speech marks.
- The identifier also ends with a comma.
- The second part of the speech sentence ends with its full stop, question mark or exclamation mark inside the speech marks.

Tick the sentences that contain the correct punctuation for speech.

- "I think," Marta said, "that the sun is coming out." ☑
- "It's no wonder you can't run," laughed Rani, "in those shoes!" ☐
- "We can barely see anything," complained Marek, "in this gloom." ☐
- "But in that case, wondered Flo, what's the point?" ☐
- "Now," demanded Eliza, "Are we in agreement?" ☐

Activity 2

> Put each of these sentences into a longer speech sentence, with an identifier in the middle.

1 If you help me, the work will take much less time.

"If you help me," said _____

2 I may be wrong, but you don't seem to be listening!

_____

3 Please would you help me climb into the boat?

_____

Activity 3

> Look back at Activity 1. Rewrite the sentences that you did **not** tick, correcting the mistakes.

_____

_____

_____

_____

_____

7: Punctuating dialogue

Activity 1

Add the correct punctuation and capital letters to this conversation. If you need to, look back at the grammar guides and activities on the last four pages.

" What ," Kerry demanded do you think you're doing

I'm trying to finish my art project Birta answered

Kerry frowned and said you're making a huge mess

Activity 2

Punctuation guide

> <u>Artu asked</u>, "What shall we do now?"
>
> "Let's watch one more episode," <u>suggested Poppy</u>.
>
> "No," <u>Helga yawned</u>, "I'm too tired."

- Dialogue is a conversation between two or more people.
- When it is written, a new line should begin every time the **speaker** changes.
- Lots of **verbs** can show that someone is speaking, not just 'to say'.
- In an <u>identifier</u>, the name of the speaker and the verb can be in either order.

Write out the dialogue in full speech sentences, using one identifier at the end of a sentence, one at the beginning and one in the middle. Try to use different verbs to show speech.

Mika: Hurry or we'll be late. Tai: We won't if Mum drives us. Mika: Wait here and I'll ask.

"Hurry _____

_____

_____

Activity 3

Write the command in a very dramatic speech sentence.
Consider the identifier's noun, verb, position and word order.

Run as quickly as you can.

_____

_____

What do I Know?

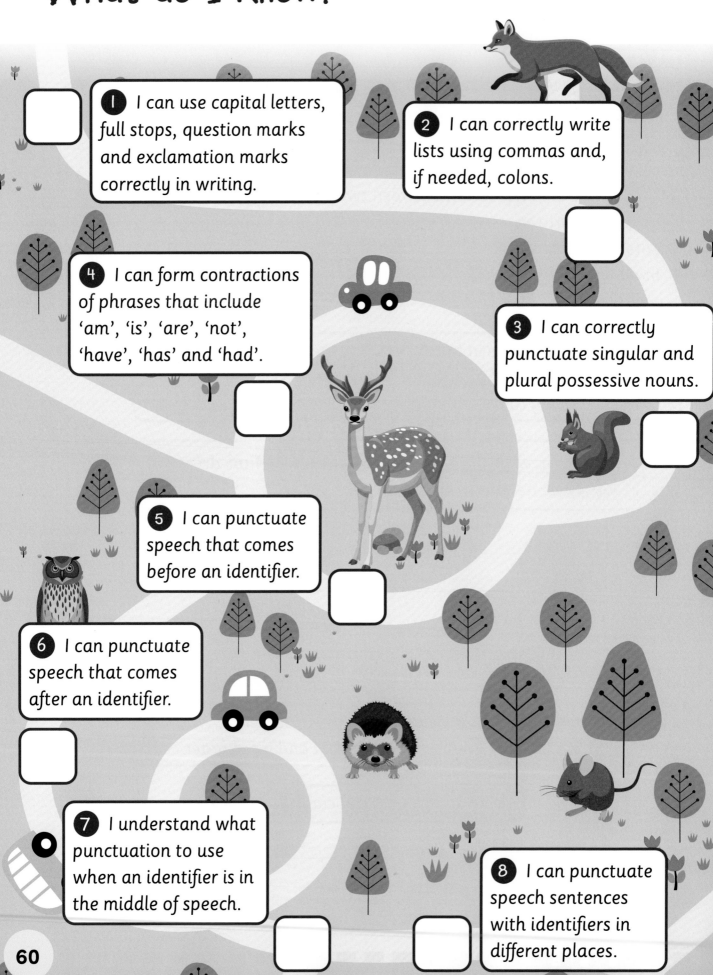

1 I can use capital letters, full stops, question marks and exclamation marks correctly in writing.

2 I can correctly write lists using commas and, if needed, colons.

4 I can form contractions of phrases that include 'am', 'is', 'are', 'not', 'have', 'has' and 'had'.

3 I can correctly punctuate singular and plural possessive nouns.

5 I can punctuate speech that comes before an identifier.

6 I can punctuate speech that comes after an identifier.

7 I understand what punctuation to use when an identifier is in the middle of speech.

8 I can punctuate speech sentences with identifiers in different places.

1: Plurals, contractions and possessives

Activity 1

Grammar guide

> The bike belonging to Rian has got flat **tyres**. It is useless at the moment, so it **stays** in the back garden of the children.
>
> Rian's **bike's** got flat **tyres**. **It's** useless at the moment, so it **stays** in the **children's** back garden.

- Adding the ending 's' to a word could mean one of several things.
- Many **plural nouns** and **third-person singular verbs** take the 's' or 'es' ending.
- **Singular possessive nouns**, and **plural possessive nouns that don't end '–s'**, take an apostrophe and then 's'.
- Contractions of '**has**' and '**is**' also take an apostrophe and then 's'.

1 Change these singular nouns into plural nouns.

a. house _____

b. box _____

c. sock _____

d. bush _____

2 Change these infinitive verbs into singular verb forms that would follow each pronoun.

a. to go She _____

b. to run He _____

c. to hope She _____

d. to buzz It _____

Activity 2

1 Rewrite these sentences, contracting all instances of 'has' and 'is'.

> Ms Tolstoy is tired because she has got trouble at home. She is looking after twelve puppies! She has hurried out of work as she is running late and the dog-sitter is strict about timing. Sometimes Ms Tolstoy has got no time to rest!

Ms Tolstoy's tired because _____

_____

_____

_____

_____

2 When 'has' is contracted, it's almost always being used as an auxiliary verb. 'Is' can be used as an auxiliary verb too. Circle the instances of 'is' being used as an auxiliary verb.

Activity 3

Change each of these phrases into a possessive noun phrase.

1 the cat belonging to Chris _____

2 the highest branch of the tree _____

3 the lunch break of the children _____

4 the hutch where the rabbit lives _____

2: Using 's' correctly

Activity 1

Grammar guide

- Adding the ending 's' to a word could mean one of several things.
- Many plural nouns and third-person singular verbs take the 's' or 'es' ending.
- Singular possessive nouns, and plural possessive nouns that don't end '–s', take an apostrophe and then 's'.
- Contractions of 'has' and 'is' also end in an apostrophe and then 's'.

Tick one box for each sentence to show why the underlined word ends '--s'.

1 She joined the <u>men's</u> golf game.
- ☐ Plural noun
- ☑ Possessive noun
- ☐ Singular verb
- ☐ Contraction

2 The <u>mugs</u> were all in the dishwasher.
- ☐ Plural noun
- ☐ Possessive noun
- ☐ Singular verb
- ☐ Contraction

3 <u>It's</u> Thursday today.
- ☐ Plural noun
- ☐ Possessive noun
- ☐ Singular verb
- ☐ Contraction

4 Next <u>door's</u> garden is overgrown.
- ☐ Plural noun
- ☐ Possessive noun
- ☐ Singular verb
- ☐ Contraction

5 <u>Mum's</u> had a cold this week.
- ☐ Plural noun
- ☐ Possessive noun
- ☐ Singular verb
- ☐ Contraction

6 Shola <u>sips</u> her juice.
- ☐ Plural noun
- ☐ Possessive noun
- ☐ Singular verb
- ☐ Contraction

Activity 2

1 Write a sentence that includes a plural noun that ends '–s'.

_____

2 Write a sentence that includes a third-person singular verb that ends '–s'.

_____

3 Write a sentence that includes a singular possessive noun.

_____

Activity 3

Grammar guide

*He's made a cake for his **sister's** party. **She's** celebrating her sixth birthday today.*

- The **contraction for 'has'** is the same as the **contraction for 'is'**.
- **Singular possessive nouns** end the same way.
- Use the context to work out the meaning of each word that ends with an apostrophe and 's'.

Rewrite the sentences, using full words instead of contractions.

Jerry's cousin's visiting from Edinburgh. Jerry's planned lots of things for them to do.

_____

_____

What do I know?

1 I understand the different uses of 's' at the ends of plural nouns, singular verbs, possessive nouns and contractions.

2 I can understand what 's' means in different sentences.

3 I can use 's' correctly at the ends of words.

Glossary

Here are some useful meanings. Key terms to understand are in orange.

Term	Meaning
Absolute adjective	An adjective that cannot have adverbials of degree such as 'more', 'very' or 'a bit' before it. For example: 'dead'; 'black'.
Adjective	A word that adds information to a noun to describe what the thing named is like. For example: 'the red dress'.
Adverbial	A word (an adverb) or phrase that adds information to an adjective, verb or other adverb. Many adverbs end '–ly', but not all of them. For example: 'I ran quickly. I was tired almost as soon as I started.'
Agreement	The way in which all the verb forms, nouns and other parts of a sentence match together in the right ways, such as in their tenses.
Alphabet	All the letters in order from A to Z. A list of words in alphabetical order starts with letters that come first in the alphabet. For example: 'apple, ball, cat …'.
Apostrophe (')	A punctuation mark that can be used to show that letters have been missed out in a contraction or to show possession. For example: 'can't'; 'the horse's ears'.
Article	The words 'a', 'an', 'the' and 'some'. They are a type of determiner.
Attributive noun	Words that function in a way similar to adjectives. They come before nouns to affect and specify meaning. However, they rarely describe what something is like but rather show what kind of thing it is, what it is for, where it is, what it is made from, or similar attributes. For example: 'car park'; 'geography teacher'.

Term	Meaning
Auxiliary verb	Words that help create different forms of verbs. Forms of the auxiliary verb 'to be' are used in progressive tenses. Forms of the auxiliary verb 'to have' are used in perfect tenses. Within these verb forms, it is the auxiliary verb that changes to show tense and person.
Capital letter	The large version of letters used at the start of a sentence or a name. Some are formed differently from the smaller letters they match. For example: 'A'; 'B'; 'C'.
Clause	A group of words, including a subject and a verb, that means one thing but is not a full sentence.
Cohesion	The way in which sentences are linked together to become effective as a whole.
Colon (:)	A punctuation mark used to introduce a reason, example, explanation or items in a list.
Comma (,)	A punctuation mark that separates items in a list and parts of a sentence that are not two clauses. It is often read as a short pause.
Command	A sentence that gives an instruction. Commands can be statements or exclamations, but they are never questions.
Compound	A word formed by joining two shorter words together. For example: super + man = superman; play + ground = playground.
Conjunction	Words that link together sentences to form one longer sentence. In the new sentence, the original sentences become known as clauses.
Consonant	Any letter that is not a vowel.
Contraction	Words that have been shortened. Apostrophes show where letters have been missed out.
Coordinating conjunction	A word that links two main clauses in a sentence.

Glossary

Term	Meaning
Definite determiner	A determiner that indicates something known and specific.
Demonstrative	The words 'this', 'that', 'these' and 'those'. They can give basic information about whether something is singular ('this' and 'that') or plural ('these' and 'those'), and nearby ('this' and 'these') or far away ('that' and 'those'). They can be used as determiners or as pronouns.
Determiner	Words, which include articles, that come before nouns. They can give basic information about whether something is singular or plural and definite or indefinite. For example: 'two boxes'; 'all of the things'.
Dialogue	A conversation between two or more people, particularly one recorded in writing.
Direct speech	Writing that reports exactly what someone says with the precise spoken words in speech marks (or 'inverted commas') and often an identifier.
Exclamation	A sudden cry that shows surprise, excitement, shock or pain and ends with an exclamation mark.
Exclamation mark (!)	A punctuation mark used at the end of a sentence, to show that the sentence is an exclamation.
Expanded noun phrase	A noun phrase that includes extra information about the thing named by the noun, for example using an adjective.
Fronted adverbial	An adverbial that comes at the start (front) of a sentence, followed by a comma. For example: 'Suddenly, there was a crash.'
Full stop (.)	A punctuation mark used at the end of a sentence, to show that the sentence is a statement.
Heading	Words that appear as titles above pieces of writing that tell the reader straight away what the piece of writing is about.
Identifier	A word that names the speaker of direct speech and includes a verb such as 'to say'. For example: "Hello," said Gunther.

Term	Meaning
Indefinite determiner	A determiner that indicates something general and non-specific.
Infinitive verb	The most basic form of a verb preceded by 'to' ('to walk'; 'to be'). It expresses no tense and no person.
Inverted commas (" "), (' ')	Punctuation marks that show speech is being reported exactly, also known as speech marks. They can be double (" ") or single (' ').
Irregular	Words that do not follow rules when they change. Verbs could have irregular tenses. Nouns could have irregular plurals.
Letter	A symbol used for writing. One group of letters makes up one word.
List	A series of connected things. For example: 'In the pond, there are fish, frogs, toads and newts.'
Main clause	The words that give the main point in a sentence. There can be more than one main clause in a sentence if they are equally important. If there are two main clauses joined by a conjunction in a sentence, swapping the order of two main clauses does not affect the meaning of the sentence.
Meaning	The thing or idea that a word, expression or sign represents.
Noun	A word that names a person, thing, event or idea.
Noun phrase	A group of words that all link to the thing named by the noun. A noun phrase could be as short as two words: a determiner and the noun.
Object	A thing or person that is not doing the action named in a sentence, but is involved in the action. For example: 'Shanice plays the game.'
Paragraph	A clear section of a piece of writing that starts on a new line, usually on one topic.
Past participle	A verb form used to form perfect tenses. A verb's past participle is usually the same as its past tense.

Term	Meaning
Past tense	A way of writing a verb to show that events or actions happened in the past.
Perfect tenses	Ways of writing a verb to show that an action is perfectly complete. They are formed with the auxiliary verb 'have', which is the verb that changes to show tense and person, and a past participle.
Person	The way in which a verb changes to show who or what does the action. Each person can be singular or plural. First-person relates to oneself (for example: 'I'; 'we'). Second person relates to the direct recipient of a sentence (for example: 'you'). Third person relates to another person or thing named in the sentence (for example: 'she'; 'the cats').
Personal pronoun	Pronouns that represent grammatical persons, including subject personal pronouns (for example: 'you'; 'they') object personal pronouns (for example: 'me'; them').
Phrase	A group of words that means something but is not a full sentence. It could be as short as two words.
Plural	A noun or pronoun that names more than one of a thing, or a verb that shows that more than one person or thing is doing the action.
Possession	Something belongs to someone or something else. This could mean it is owned by them or is related to them in a different way.
Possessive noun	A noun that shows possession. The noun for the owner takes the possessive form. For singular nouns and plurals that do not end '–s', this is made up of the noun, an apostrophe and 's'. For plural nouns that end '–s', it is made up of the noun and an apostrophe.
Possessive pronoun	A word that stands in for a possessive noun. Possessive pronouns can be determiners (for example: 'my'; 'your') or they can be used independently, to mean the possessive noun and the thing that is owned (for example: 'mine'; 'yours').
Prefix	A group of letters added at the start of a word to change its meaning. For example: unhappy; replay.

Term	Meaning
Preposition	A word that makes links between parts of a sentence. It usually comes at the beginning of a prepositional phrase (for example: 'up the street'; 'around the bend'; 'with a big smile'; 'after lunch'). They can be parts of a noun phrase (for example: 'I live in the house up the street') or they can be adverbials (for example: 'I live up the street').
Present participle	A verb form ending '–ing', used to form progressive tenses.
Present tense	A way of writing a verb to show that events or actions happen now or happen regularly.
Progressive tenses	Ways of writing a verb to show that an action continues over a period of time. They are formed with the auxiliary verb 'is', which is the verb that changes to show tense and person, and a present participle.
Pronoun	A word that stands in for a noun or noun phrase. The words 'I', 'you' singular, 'he', 'she', 'it', 'we', 'you' plural and 'they' are all pronouns.
Punctuation	Marks that are not letters used in writing to make the meaning easier to understand.
Quantitative determiner	Words that give information about quantity. For example: 'all'; 'some'; 'every'; three'.
Question	A sentence that is used to ask for information. It ends with a question mark.
Question mark (?)	A punctuation mark used at the end of a sentence, in place of a full stop, to show that a sentence is a question.
Sentence	A group of words that means one whole thing. It gives a whole idea.
Singular	A noun or pronoun that names only one thing, or a verb that shows that one person or thing is doing the action.
Speech marks (" "), (' ')	Punctuation marks that show speech is being reported exactly, also known as inverted commas. They can be double (" ") or single (' ').

Term	Meaning
Standard English	English that is grammatically correct.
Statement	A sentence that gives a piece of information and ends with a full stop rather than a question mark or an exclamation mark.
Sub-heading	Titles that are smaller than headings. They appear before shorter sections within a piece of writing and can help guide a reader through the text.
Subject	The person or thing doing the action in a sentence. The subject carries out the action named by the verb.
Subordinate clause	A group of words that gives extra information that is not the key point in a sentence. There cannot be a subordinate clause in a sentence without a main clause. If a main clause and a subordinate clause are joined by a conjunction in a sentence, swapping their positions affects the meaning or makes no sense.
Subordinating conjunction	A word that links a main clause to a subordinate clause in a sentence.
Suffix	A letter or group of letters added at the end of a word to change its meaning. For example: farming; farmer.
Tense	The way in which a verb shows when the action happens.
Verb	A word that names an action. Every sentence must contain at least one verb.
Vowel	The letters 'a', 'e', 'i', 'o' and 'u'.
Word	A group of letters that make up one unit of meaning. In writing, a word has a space on each side of it. In slow speech, a word has a short silence on each side of it.
Word family	A group of words with the same root word and related spellings. For example: 'farm', 'farmer', 'farming' and 'farmed'; 'please', 'displeasing', 'pleasant' and 'pleasantries'.

Determiners and pronouns

1: Simple determiners

Activity 1

Some of the [circled]
each [underlined]
A few [circled]
that [underlined]
one [underlined]
A [circled]
the [underlined]

Activity 2

- **Some of the**: There's more than one door but not all have alarms.
- **each**: There's more than one window and all of them are locked.
- **A few**: More than one window has an alarm, but not all of them.
- **that**: The skylight is singular and far away. There could be others somewhere else.
- **one**: He saw more than one corridor but he means only one of them.
- **A**: He isn't talking about a specific jump.
- **the**: There is only one roof.

[Children may use different wordings, but comprehension of each determiner's implications must be correct.]

Activity 3

[Children's answers will vary, but each must be five appropriate determiners.]

2: Personal pronouns

Activity 1

Subject pronouns:
I; you; he; she; it; we; you; they
Object pronouns:
me; you; him; her; it; us; you; them

Activity 2

I; the train; It; it; He; us; he; They; we; us

[Children's answers may vary a little, but each must be a clear and non-repetitive passage with correct pronouns chosen.]

Activity 3

1. The girl [underlined]; she [circled]
2. The sound of the crowd [underlined]; It [circled]
3. My brother [underlined]; him [circled]

3: Demonstrative determiners

Activity 1

1. that [underlined]; definite [ticked]; singular [ticked]; far [ticked]
2. This [underlined]; definite [ticked]; singular [ticked]; near [ticked]
3. those [underlined]; definite [ticked]; plural [ticked]; far [ticked]
4. These [underlined]; definite [ticked]; plural [ticked]; near [ticked]

Activity 2

1a. this; 1b. those; 1c. these; 1d. that
2a. those; 2b. this; 2c. That; 2d. these

Activity 3

1–4. [Children's answers will vary, but each must be a noun phrase including a demonstrative determiner not used elsewhere in the activity.]

4: Demonstrative pronouns

Activity 1

1. these
2. those
3. this
4. that

Activity 2

1a. that [underlined]; getting flowers

1b. This [underlined]; the karate lesson [Children's wordings may vary, but comprehension of the determiner's implications must be correct.]

1c. That [underlined]; the idea that good things come to those who wait [Children's wordings may vary, but comprehension of the determiner's implications must be correct.]

2a. This

2b. That

Activity 3

[Children's answers will vary, but each must be two sentences, the second starting with 'This' or 'That' as a reference to to the idea in the first.]

5: Possessive determiners

Activity 1

1. our; 2. my, his; 3. your, her; 4. their, its

Activity 2

1. their opinions
2. its basic ideas
3. our friends
4. your desk

Activity 3

[Children's answers will vary, but each must be three sentences that use three different possessive determiners.]

6: Independent possessive pronouns

Activity 1

- hers: Velma's model
- theirs: the twins' model
- yours: the twins' model
- ours: the twins' model
- mine: Jo's idea (for the model)
- his: Vicente's idea (for the model)

Activity 2

1. We hung our paintings, but theirs aren't dry yet.
2. I've lost my book. Can I borrow yours?
3. Your lunch looks tastier than ours.
4. She drank her tea, but his was too hot.

Activity 3

[Children's answers will vary, but each must use the possessive pronoun 'mine'.]

7: Creating clarity and cohesion

Activity 1

1. [Children's answers will vary, but each must be a quantitative determiner (but not a number) indicating plural items, such as 'several', 'some' or 'a few'.]
2. those
3. his / your

Activity 2

[Children's answers will vary, but each must be a non-repetitive paragraph that includes at least three different kinds of pronoun: subject personal, object personal, demonstrative, relative and/or possessive.]

Activity 3

[Children's answers will vary, but their responses to Activity 2 should be annotated (if necessary) to avoid repetition and ensure clarity.]

Verb forms for Standard English

1: What do you remember about verb forms?

Activity 1

is; is; says; going; done; had; forgot [each circled]

Activity 2

1. have [circled]; hurried [underlined]; present perfect
2. was [circled]; hurrying [underlined]; past progressive
3. am [circled]; hurrying [underlined]; present progressive
4. had [circled]; hurried [underlined]; past perfect

Activity 3

- Where have you been? [ticked]
- The days are getting shorter. [ticked]
- has [circled]
- They were getting fed up. [ticked]
- has [circled]
- Nami had heard the story. [ticked]
- were [circled]
- are [circled]

2: Creating Standard English

Activity 1

1. am   2. am   3. said   4. go
5. do   6. has   7. forget

Activity 2

1a. had
1b. have / has
1c. am / are / is
1d. was / were
2. Progressive: Present participle [ticked] [Children's answers will vary, but each must be a present participle.]

Perfect: Past participle [ticked] [Children's answers will vary, but each must be a past participle.]

Activity 3

My cousin Yael is training as a dancer. He goes to a ballet school. Before he applied, he had practised every day. Now the practice has worked: he is living his dream. We were hoping to watch him perform last week.

More expanded noun phrases

1: Exploring adjectives

Activity 1

1. friendly; loud; booming; long, refreshing; great [each underlined]
2. [Children's answers will vary, but each must observe the rules about commas between adjectives.]

Activity 2

1. The farmer cared for the fluffy white lambs. [ticked]
2. Under the bridge, Sala saw a big, slimy, smelly troll. [ticked]
3. We tried to take a photo of the stunning green bird. [ticked]
4. It was a completely unexpected, utterly astonishing sight. [ticked]
5. There was a clear blue sky overhead. [ticked]

Activity 3

[Children's answers will vary, but each must observe the rules about commas and absolute verbs.]

2: Adding extra nouns

Activity 1
family; ice-cream; sea; sand

Activity 2
1. Attributive noun [ticked]
2. Adjective [ticked]
3. Adjective [ticked]
4. Attributive noun [ticked]

Activity 3
school; tennis; car; music

3: Exploring prepositional phrases

Activity 1
1. Adverbial [ticked]
2. Part of a noun phrase [ticked]
3. Part of a noun phrase [ticked]
4. Adverbial [ticked]

Activity 2
1. cause
2. time
3. quality
4. place

Activity 3
[Children's answers will vary, but they must include a prepositional phrase showing:
1. place
2. quality
3. time.]

4: Expanding noun phrases

Activity 1
1. Attributive noun [ticked]
2. Adjective; Prepositional phrase [each ticked]
3. Adjective; Attributive noun [each ticked]
4. Prepositional phrase [ticked]

Activity 2
[Children's answers will vary, but each must expand the noun phrase in a way not used in the other questions: with an adjective, an attributive noun or a prepositional phrase.]

Activity 3
[Children's answers will vary, but each must include three noun phrases expanded in different ways: with an adjective, an attributive noun and a prepositional phrase.]

Fronted adverbials

1: Exploring adverbials

Activity 1
1. loudly [underlined]
2. at 11 o'clock [underlined] [ticked]
3. often [underlined]
4. only outside [underlined]

Activity 2
1a. probability 1b. cause 1c. frequency;
1d. manner 1e. time 1f. number;
1g. degree 1h. place
2. d; e; h

Activity 3
Controlling her fear; slowly; as it swung away; in front of her; into the blackness; Every now and again; from below her; only once; so she could finally go home [each underlined]

2: Adding adverbials for effect

Activity 1
1. There was suddenly a loud noise.
2. [Children's answers will vary, but each should add an adverb.]
3. [Children's answers will vary, but each should add an adverbial phrase.]

Activity 2

1. The dish fell with a clatter.
2. [Children's answers will vary, but each must add an adverbial that gives detail about probability.]
3. [Children's answers will vary, but each must add an adverbial that gives detail about frequency.]
4. [Children's answers will vary, but each must add an adverbial that gives detail about degree.]

Activity 3

1. [Children's answers will vary, but each must be a sentence that includes a labelled adverbial.]
2. [Children's answers will vary, but each must be a sentence that includes a labelled adverbial that gives a different kind of detail from the adverbial used in answer to Question 1.]

3: What are fronted adverbials?

Activity 1

- After finishing our exams, my friends and I went camping. [ticked]
- As the sun rose, the birds began to sing. [ticked]
- With surprise, I wondered how he could have run so quickly. [ticked]

Activity 2

1a. We need to know not to nod straight away.
1b. We need to know to be careful with the egg yolks before putting them in.
2a. It helps us to imagine the crash.
2b. It helps us to imagine the scene.

[Children's answers will vary, but each should note effects similar to the ones above.]

Activity 3

[Children's answers will vary, but each should acknowledge that fronted adverbials establish context before action.]

4: Conjunctions in fronted adverbials

Activity 1

- When the clock struck twelve, she hurried home. [ticked]
- If you promise to return it, you can use my coat. [ticked]
- So I didn't ruin the surprise, I closed my eyes tightly. [ticked]

Activity 2

1. [Children's answers will vary, but each sentence must include a main clause, a subordinating conjunction and then a subordinate clause.]
2. [Each answer should rearrange a sentence written in Question 1 to use the conjunctions and subordinate clauses as fronted adverbials.]

Activity 3

- Although I really want to see you, I'm not free today.
- So he didn't trip over, Suni turned on his torch.
- When the sun rose, Chloë woke up.

5: Adding fronted adverbials

Activity 1

1a. Immediately, there was a reaction.
1b. So she wasn't late, she ran all the way home.
1c. In the mirror, I saw someone else.
2. Preposition: C
   Subordinating conjunction: B

Activity 2

1. Yesterday, I saw my friends.
[2–4. Children's answers will vary, but each must add a fronted adverbial that gives detail about: 2. place; 3. cause; 4. number.]

Activity 3

[Children's answers will vary, but each must use a fronted adverbial intended to create mystery.]

6: Forming topical paragraphs

Activity 1

- In France: Setting
- The next summer: Time
- For ordinary people: Topic

Activity 2

[Children's answers will vary, but each must complete two topically coherent paragraphs (of two or three sentences) on what they do in the morning and what they do in the evening, respectively.]

Activity 3

[Children's answers will vary, but each must be a topically coherent paragraph beginning with a relevant fronted adverbial.]

Punctuation

1: Revising sentence punctuation

Activity 1

1. [Children's answers will vary, but each must be a statement labelled to show its verb, capital letter, subject noun, object noun and punctuation.]
2. [Children's answers will vary, but each must change the statement written for Question 1 to a correctly formed question.]

Activity 2

[Children's answers will vary, but each must include at least one statement, one exclamation, one question and one command.]

Activity 3

[Children's answers will vary, but each must correct any mistakes in their answer to Question 1.]

2: Exploring lists

Activity 1

1. I hurried home, got changed and went to meet my friends.
2. [Children's answers will vary, but each must be a full sentence that includes a correctly punctuated list of the given nouns. For example: 'In my garden, there are blackbirds, crows, pigeons and sparrows.']

Activity 2

1a–b. [Children's answers will vary, but each must complete the list with three actions.]
2. [Children's answers will vary, but each must introduce the list with a main clause and a colon.]

Activity 3

Sammy watched TV, ate her dinner and went to bed. [ticked]
This is how I learn a spelling: look at it, cover it, write it and check it. [ticked]

3: Revising possessive apostrophes

Activity 1

- A footpath crosses our school's playing field. [ticked]
- The bus's doors opened slowly. [ticked]

- Our trees' leaves were turning golden brown. [ticked]
- The women's ideas solved the problem. [ticked]

Activity 2

1. The dog's bowl is empty.
[2–4. Children's answers will vary, but each must include the possessive noun phrase written: 2. Elias's books; 3. the houses' doors; 4. the sheep's wool.]

Activity 3

- People's differences are important.
- Smoke billowed from both of the cars' engines.
- Lida's friends were waiting for her.
- The circus's posters are all over town.

4: Exploring contractions

Activity 1

I'm annoyed that I can't see the performances Hallie's in. They're during my holiday. It's such a shame.

Activity 2

1. I've arrived. He's arrived. We've arrived. They'd arrived.
2. They'd hated the painting I've now displayed, but it's attracted a lot of attention.

Activity 3

[Children's answers will vary, but each must include at least four different contractions.]

5: Revising direct speech

Activity 1

- "Could you clean up?" asked my mum. [ticked]
- Mum replied, "You go out a lot!" [ticked]

Activity 2

1a. Kris said, "It's so beautiful."
1b. Kris said, "You'd love it here!"
2a. "I am waiting," Ama said.
2b. "Where are you?" Ama asked.
[Children's choices of identifiers may vary in verb, noun and word order, but their positions should be accurate.]

Activity 3

- "I was planning to go out," I said.
- "I'm helping Kenta with her homework!" I cried.
- I said, "I'll clean up quickly first."

6: Another way to write speech

Activity 1

- "I think," Marta said, "that the sun is coming out." [ticked]
- "It's no wonder you can't run," laughed Rani, "in those shoes!" [ticked]
- "We can barely see anything," complained Marek, "in this gloom." [ticked]

Activity 2

1. "If you help me," said [X], "the work will take much less time."
2. "I may be wrong," said [X], "but you don't seem to be listening!"
3. "Please," said [X], "would you help me climb into the boat?"
[Children's answers will vary in their choice of identifier and, for Question 3, where in the sentence they put it.]

Activity 3

- "But in that case," wondered Flo, "what's the point?"
- "Now," demanded Eliza, "are we in agreement?"

7: Punctuating dialogue

Activity 1
"What," Kerry demanded, "do you think you're doing?"

"I'm trying to finish my art project," Birta answered.

Kerry frowned and said, "You're making a huge mess."

Activity 2
[Children's answers will vary, but each must be three full speech sentences that position one identifier at the beginning of a sentence, one at the end and one in the middle.]

Activity 3
[Children's answers will vary, but each must be a correctly formed speech sentence composed with an intention to create drama.]

Understanding 's'

1: Plurals, contractions and possessives

Activity 1
1a. houses; 1b. boxes; 1c. socks; 1d. bushes

2a. goes; 2b. runs; 2c. hopes; 2d. buzzes

Activity 2
1. Ms Tolstoy's tired because she's got trouble at home. She's looking after twelve puppies! She's hurried out of work as she's running late and the dog-sitter's strict about timing. Sometimes Ms Tolstoy's got no time to rest!

2. [The instances of 'is' in the following phrases should be circled in the extract.]
She is looking; she is running

Activity 3
1. Chris's cat
2. the tree's highest branch
3. the children's lunch break
4. the rabbit's hutch

2: Using 's' correctly

Activity 1
1. Possessive noun [ticked]
2. Plural noun [ticked]
3. Contraction [ticked]
4. Possessive noun [ticked]
5. Contraction [ticked]
6. Singular verb [ticked]

Activity 2
1. [Children's answers will vary, but each must be a sentence including a plural noun that ends '–s'.]
2. [Children's answers will vary, but each must be a sentence including a third-person singular verb that ends '–s'.]
3. [Children's answers will vary, but each must be a sentence including a singular possessive noun.]

Activity 3
Jerry's cousin is visiting from Edinburgh. Jerry has planned lots of things for them to do.

My notes

My notes